Shooting Stars

Melvin and Gilda Berger

SCHOLASTIC INC.
New York Toronto London Auckland Sydney
Mexico City New Delhi Hong Kong Buenos Aires

Photographs: Cover: Astrofoto/Shigemi Numazawa/Peter Arnold, Inc.;
p. 1: Astrofoto/Shigemi Numazawa/Peter Arnold, Inc.;
p. 3: Astrofoto/Shigemi Numazawa/Peter Arnold, Inc.;
p. 4: ESA, NASA/Dembinsky Photo Assoc.;
p. 5: Astrofoto/Shigemi Numazawa/Peter Arnold, Inc.;
p. 6: Frank Whitney/The Image Bank/Getty Images;
p. 7: Astrofoto/Olivier Staiger/Peter Arnold, Inc.;
p. 8: Astrofoto/Shigemi Numazawa/Peter Arnold, Inc.;
p. 9: Kauko Helavuo/The Image Bank/Getty Images;
p. 10: Astrofoto/Keller/Schmidbauer/Peter Arnold, Inc.;
p. 11: Pekka Parviainen/Dembinsky Photo Assoc.;
p. 12: Astrofoto/van Ravenswaay/Peter Arnold, Inc.; p. 13: Scholastic Photo Library;
p. 14: Pete Turner/The Image Bank/Getty Images; p. 15: NASA;
p. 16: Astrofoto/Motomaro Shirao/Peter Arnold, Inc.

*The paintings in this book are artists' representations of the planets and do not always show
the rings around Jupiter, Uranus, and Neptune. The rings around Saturn are always shown.*

Photo Research: Sarah Longacre

ISBN 0-439-57480-3

12 11 10 9 8 7 6 5 4 3 2   4 5 6 7 8 9/0
08

Printed in the U.S.A.
First printing, January 2004

Shooting stars are not stars.

Shooting stars are bits
of rock or iron.

They are part of
the solar system.

Shooting stars fall from space toward Earth.

They make streaks
of light in the sky.

Some streaks of light are short.

Some streaks of light are long.

Fun Fact

Most shooting stars are smaller than grains of sand.

Most shooting stars
burn up in the air.

They fall to Earth as dust.

Fun Fact

When a shooting star lands on Earth it is called a meteorite.

Some shooting stars land on Earth.

Big ones can make big holes.

Some nights have a
few shooting stars.

Some nights have many shooting stars.

How many shooting
stars do you see?